Sheila Ruiz Harrell

Let's Make Authentic *Californio* Tamales!

and *Sarsa*!

Copyright © 2026 Sheila Ruiz Harrell
All rights reserved.

The information in this book does not, and is not intended to, constitute any kind of professional advice. To the maximum extent permitted by law, the author does not guarantee the accuracy or completeness of the information presented in this book, and specifically disclaims any implied warranties of merchantability or fitness for a particular purpose. The author shall not be liable for any loss of profit or any other damages, including but not limited to special, incidental, consequential, personal, or other damages. The author is not responsible for the outcome of any recipe in this book. You may not achieve desired results due to differences in areas such as ingredients, cooking temperatures, or your individual cooking ability.

Published in the United States and the United Kingdom
by WingSpan Press, Livermore, CA

The WingSpan name, logo and colophon are the trademarks of WingSpan Publishing.

ISBN 978-1-63683-077-3 (pbk.)
ISBN 978-1-63683-935-6 (ebk.)

First ebook edition January 2026

All trademarks, service marks, logos, and brand names are the property of their respective owners and do not constitute or imply sponsorship or endorsement of this book or author by those owners.

Sheila Ruiz Harrell
Sheila@CalifornioAncestry.com

Printed in the United States of America
www.wingspanpress.com

Acknowledgements

How can I possibly thank all the people involved in the creation of this book, these recipes, of our *Californio* tamales? I'm not sure how, but I'm going to try!

My *abuelos y abuelas*, my grandfathers and grandmothers several generations before me, chose to come to this unknown land (now California) to begin new lives. With them they brought the recipes and knowledge of how to make our *Californio* tamales, and they brought *sarsa*!

I never met my *abuelas* from the families of Bojórques, Galindo, Durán, López, Sinova, Pinto, Fernández, Pico, Valenzuela, Moreno, Cordero, and Ruiz, all born before 1850, before California became a state. But they shared their cooking skills with me through the years—I've felt all of them in my kitchens as I cooked.

My two maternal great-grandmas, the one from my mother's father's side of my family and the other one from my mother's mother's side, each had a huge influence on my cooking. The utensils I've used, handed down to me that belonged to them, have delivered their energy to me while I was at my stove. They're with me.

These two women, my maternal great-grandmothers, tried their best to pass on their knowledge, skills, the expertise of making the *Californio* tamales, but sigh, my mother just didn't absorb any of it! Mom wasn't a big fan of Mexican-style food, although that's about all that was served in her house while growing up! Mom wasn't a big fan of cooking in general, but she filled our kitchen with great food! She just didn't like to cook. I love to cook!! My *abuelas* were strong and their spirits passed to me were stronger!

My mother's mother, my *abuela*, Nana as I called her, gave me my very best, and very first memories of food! Nana's kitchen always smelled of cumin, oregano, and chiles! Nana made delicious tortillas!

Nana has been in my kitchen whenever I cook the beans, and the rice, the enchiladas, and of course, the *Californio* tamales—and *sarsa*! Nana hasn't been with me physically because she died when I was just 13, but Nana is always with me in spirit. She was with me as I made my first *Californio* tamales, and when I served them the first time to my mother. Mom said they were just like her Mama made!

Best compliment ever!

I thank my husband, Al, for all the time he's spent in the kitchen with me as we made so many of our *Californio* tamales. And for the time he's spent cleaning and crunching dried chili peppers, and sorting the corn husks, and cutting then shredding the meat, and he kept the dishes and utensils washed and dried, and all the other bazillion things he's done for me as we made our *Californio* tamales. It's not a one-person job, it takes teamwork! We make ours as a team of two!!

I also thank my brother Mike for our shopping trips to find the perfect peppers and corn husks, and for the times he cleaned those peppers for me. Mike didn't wear gloves once and much later in the day he changed his contact lenses . . . and had several painful hours afterwards!

I'm also thanking my two children, Virginia and Richard, and my three grandchildren, Peter, Nicole, and Greggory, for being my taste-testers! I don't think they minded having that job over the years!

And of course, there would be no book without the tireless work of my great friend and co-author of our *Californio* Ancestry website (CalifornioAncestry.com), Don Gibson. This book has not been easy, but Don made it seem so.

Un fuerte abrazo y mucho amor.

Contents

Acknowledgements iii
Introduction 1
Let's get ready 4
    What are *Californio* tamales? 5
    Tamale tips—do this, not that 8
    Ingredients you can't do without 11
    Equipment required 13
Let's start cooking! 16
    Chile pepper purée 17
    Creating the BEST sauce 20
    Preparing the meat mixture 23
    Corn husks—or *hojas de maiz* 26
    Mixing the masa—the fluffy, blushing tamale dough 28
    Pennnies in the pot? Dancing pennies? 32
    Tamalada—tamales-building time! 34
    Serving and eating *Californio* tamales 41
    Bonus recipe: vegan tamales and their own sauce 43
    Californio sarsa 49
About the author 52

Introduction

When my ancestors arrived here in 1776 (yes, that's Seventeen seventy-six!) to the future lands of California, they brought many things from their old life to make their life in the new, unknown place seem more like home. One of the things they brought with them was their method of making tamales. This method has been passed down from our ancestors through so many of the early *Californio* families. No, that wasn't a typo, the word is "Californi-o", with an "o", not an "a" on the end of it.

The *Californios* were the first non-native people who permanently settled today's California; they were the Spanish-speaking subjects of the King of Spain, coming from the area now known as México in *Nueva España* (New Spain). My *Californio* ancestors moved to, or were born in, or grew up in what is now the State of California, between 1769 and the signing of the Treaty of Guadalupe Hidalgo on February 2, 1848, when California became a territory of the United States.

I am a 7th generation *Californio*—six generations before me, all born IN pre- or post-statehood California! I have deep *Californio* roots!

So, we're going to make *Californio*-style tamales.

This word "style" doesn't mean the tamales aren't authentic, it just means that my grandmas and I have tweaked the recipes a bit and updated them through the years, mostly just in the methods of making them. We now use an electric mixer instead of a wooden spoon! We use a blender to make the sauce smooth and *delicioso*! And we buy packages of *hojas para tamales*, or corn husks, for our tamales instead of gathering the husks.

And we use a handy-dandy tool to tie the ends of the tamales, instead of using two people to tie one *tamal*!

Yes, I said *tamal*, not tamales. One is a *tamal* but the word tamales describes more than one of these steaming-hot, delicious bundles of meat, masa, and sauce. Quite possibly the best thing you've ever eaten.

We make basic tamales, nothing really unusual, other than we've added vegan tamales for a special person in our family.

We make a combination of pork and beef tamales, or all beef for our non-pork eating family members and friends. We also make vegetable and black bean tamales as our vegan tamales.

Originally, we used lard in the masa, but we now use shortening for our non-pork and vegan family members and friends.

My mother was never very interested in her *Californio* lineage, or in learning to cook the foods of our ancestors, but I was, always.

When I was a very small child, my parents and I lived with my Nana and Papa, my mother's parents. By age four I followed my Nana around her kitchen listening to every word she was telling me. I watched in wonderment as she turned a bowl of dry flour and a few other things into round white balls that had to sit on the kitchen table, resting under a big dish towel until

Nana did a funny thing with her hands—flap, flap, flap and put the large and flimsy white thing on the stove. The indescribable deliciousness that came off the stove moments later had me dancing around the kitchen! Nana would slather the very thin, large hot tortilla with creamy butter, plop me in a chair, and watch my face light up as I bit into the creation beyond words! There is nothing like a warm, butter-slathered tortilla fresh off the stove! It's messy. It drips melted butter down your arms. It gets on your clothes when you're just a little kid. But there's just nothing like it.

My mother was never very pleased with the mess I made, but the warm buttered tortilla that Nana had just made was always worth it!

Fast forward to me in my forties and finally making a Christmas Eve tamale dinner for my parents, siblings and their spouses, my adult children and spouses, plus my grandchildren. The tamales and beans were made at my home to be heated at Mom's place. I made the rice there while everything else was heating and the other family members were setting the table. I was a bit nervous. This was the great reveal—MY tamales, presented to Mom.

After we all said grace, raised our glasses with "*saludos amigos*" and "*Feliz Navidad*" ("greetings friends" and "Merry Christmas"), the food was passed around and there was a lot of chatter. And then there was silence.

Mom took a bite of her tamale, then another bite, and then in an almost excited whisper, she said "These taste just like Mama used to make! How did you do that?!" And that was the BEST compliment I could have received!

Let's get started. Let's make authentic *Californio* tamales!

Let's Get Ready

A few brief chapters to get you prepared for making authentic *Californio* tamales

CHAPTER 1

What Are *Californio* Tamales?

Yes, let's get started. Let's make authentic *Californio* tamales! But wait! Before we begin, I want you to know something about these tamales, these *Californio*-style tamales.

I know, you can easily learn about how tamales came to be, and when and where they were first made and eaten. You can learn all about them online, but you won't learn about my families' tamales.

When my great-grandparents were growing up near the California missions of Santa Barbara and Santa Clara, their families were large, and they owned many acres of land. They celebrated the Christmas holiday by hosting huge *tamaladas*, tamale-making parties! Often even the children helped, or just had fun running all around with their many *primos* (cousins).

All of that was when California was still new. New to being the State of California. But in a few more years, maybe in a few generations, when the newness was worn away, my great-grandparents found themselves living such different lives.

Papa's parents owned acres of beautiful land in Santa Barbara County. Papa's father was a successful stock-raiser.

Nana's mother's family owned property at San José in Santa Clara County, and then in Watsonville and Pájaro, in Santa Cruz County.

And then these families didn't own much of anything.

Nana's family moved from the shanties near the Pájaro River to the western part of Fresno County, much more inland to escape the violence of Santa Cruz County.

Papa's father's land was drying up due to the drought of those years, and his stock was dying so he packed up his family, his wife, two almost-grown daughters, and two young sons, and walked from Sisquoc in Santa Barbara County to the newly-developed town of Madera, in the new county of Madera—named for the abundance of wood and the lumber mill. Papa's father knew there was work in the mill. His father-in-law was already working there along with a few of his wife's brothers. It was a long walk for his family and his few remaining livestock. The year was 1900.

Nana's parents were raising her and her siblings in the tiny town of Firebaugh in west Fresno County. Mr. Henry Miller owned most of the land and almost all of the cattle, sheep, and even pigs in the area. He also owned most of the town, but he employed almost all the male residents and paid a good wage. The year was 1900.

Papa's family was in Madera and Nana's family was in Firebaugh, about 25 miles apart, and eventually the two would meet and marry. But before that happened, life took a different turn.

Papa's mother was very frail, and ill. With the help of her nearly-grown daughters, they made tamales like those made generations earlier. The *Californio* tamales. Papa's family celebrated Christmas with *tamaladas* and all the happy laughter of the season as the families came together to make tamales!

Meanwhile, in Firebaugh, Nana's family was doing much the same celebrating. Nana was related to so many folks in the town so when they held *tamaladas*, it was a huge party!!

For both Papa's family and Nana's family, those early years of the 1900s were a struggle to put food on the table and pay the bills. In the past, making tamales was for celebrations— weddings, baptisms, holidays—but now the *tamaladas* were for individual families, making tamales to pay the bills.

There were times in Firebaugh when small children would take buckets of fresh tamales around the affluent neighborhoods to sell, to try to pay the bills.

Today when I smell the deliciousness of the steaming tamales, I am immediately taken back to my very early childhood at Nana and Papa's home, and I can see all the smiling faces of family members with all the loud laughter, and I feel the love, and I know how our *Californio*-style tamales kept the families going through the bad times—and how they helped pay the bills!

So now, let's get started. Let's make authentic *Californio* tamales because everybody loves tamales!

CHAPTER 2

Tamale Tips—Do This, Not That

Throughout these instructions we point out some cautions—things to watch out for or be careful of, such as the steam from the tamale pot (I've burned my arm with this and it hurt for a week!).

Look for this icon for the caution statements:

We also have several hints and tips to help your tamale-making be as successful as possible.

Look for this icon for the hints and tips:

After gathering all of the ingredients needed, and all of the equipment required, there are a few steps to do right at the beginning.

1) Put a few pennies (we use 3) in the bottom of the tamale

steamer, or whatever pot that will be used to steam the tamales. Fill the tamale steamer with cold water to just below the rack used to keep the tamales out of the water. There is a marked line a couple of inches above the bottom of the pot on a tamale pot which is the water level line. We set this up before starting the assembling of the tamales so everything is ready when the tamales are wrapped and tied.

2) Check the bucket or container used for soaking the husks for leaks. Yes, we've had this happen, so check it first.

3) Wipe down all surfaces the husks will be touching with something like disinfecting wipes, or spray with a disinfectant and allow to air-dry before use. The wide, inside husk will be in contact with the masa on the second husk, so it needs to be on a clean surface.

4) Wear clean aprons. We put on our aprons when we enter the kitchen to work on the tamales to both protect our clothing, but also to keep our workspace as sanitary as possible. When we need to leave the kitchen (maybe to use the bathroom), we remove our aprons, do what we need to do, then return to the kitchen, wash our hands (again!), and put on our aprons. This may sound very bossy, and almost preaching to you, but we don't know your habits or knowledge of how germs are spread. This is just FYI.

5) Anything dropped on the floor is to be replaced—masa spreader, scoop, husk, etc.

6) Be aware that you'll be washing dishes ALL day! Maybe not actual dishes but all the measuring utensils, spoons, spatulas, etc. will need to be washed repeatedly before moving to the next step.

7) That's it, let's do this thing!!

Californio Tamales! and Sarsa!

Wait a minute!

You really need to understand the steps to this somewhat lengthy, and a bit labor intensive process.

Making tamales will take at least two days, probably three days, from start to finish.

This tamale making is NOT something you would do the same day as guests would be arriving for dinner!

First clean the chile peppers, then soak and purée them in a blender.

Cut the meat into cubes, sear (brown) the meat, then boil it until very tender. AFTER the purée is made and the meat is cooked, the husks can then be rinsed and soaked for at least an hour.

While the husks are soaking, the masa can be made, and then the husks are sorted by size.

Masa is spread on the husk, and the meat mixture added along with the olive and three raisins.

The person doing the wrapping ties the tails and, ta-da!, the *tamal* is made and ready for the steamer.

Finally, about 2 hours later, with an intoxicating aroma wafting through the room, the *tamal* is delicately unwrapped, exposing the wonderfully fluffy masa and deliciously seasoned meat mixture. Dive in! You deserve it!!

CHAPTER 3

Ingredients You Can't Do Without

Gather these first before beginning the tamale-making! Then check your supplies again! Items can be so easily overlooked and then bring the whole process to a complete stop when you're scrambling to find the missing item!

Servings:
24 tamales

Key ingredients:
- 2.5 pounds pork—we use boneless Boston butt roasts
- 1.5 pounds beef—we use boneless chuck roasts
- 1 bag (4.4 lbs) masa—we use Maseca brand Instant Corn Masa Mix for Tamales (**not the cornmeal for tortillas!**)
- 1 pound or 1 package corn husks
- 10 California chile peppers, dried
- 6 Pasilla chile peppers, dried
- 1 garlic clove
- 1 pound shortening—we use Crisco brand instead of lard

- cornstarch
- baking powder
- salt & pepper—we use McCormick brand Montreal Steak Seasoning for a good blend
- 12.5 cups (100 fl oz) chicken broth—we use Swanson brand
- apple cider vinegar
- ground oregano
- ground cumin
- ground ancho chile
- garlic powder
- 1 can black olives, pitted (you only need 24 but a can allows for eating some, too!)
- 1 package raisins (you only need 72, but a package allows for snacking!)

CHAPTER 4
Equipment Required

Be certain you have every piece of equipment set out before you begin. It's so frustrating to need a spatula or whisk and it's still in the dishwasher or drawer, anywhere but where you need it to be!

- electric mixer—a hand-mixer works best
- a very large bowl, bigger than the bowl on a stand mixer
- sharp knife
- measuring cups (¼, 2, 4, and 8 cup sizes)
- measuring spoons
- mixing spoons
- spatulas
- whisk
- ice cream scoop
- tongs
- large strainer
- 2 to 3 quart saucepan
- large frying pan or sauté pan
- large pot—soup pot, stew pot, kettle, or something similar

- large steamer pot or a tamale pot
- large container to soak corn husks, maybe a bucket?
- 1 quart storage container, with a lid
- many towels—cloth kitchen towels for drying corn husks
- paper towels—for wiping hands and spills, not for use on corn husks!
- food-grade gloves
- food-grade cotton kitchen string
- baking sheets or trays
- food scale
- blender—we use our Vita-Mix
- 3 pennies to dance at the bottom of the tamale pot
- *Tamal* Tying Tool, a.k.a. Handy-Dandy Tying Tool (optional)

Here's how to make the *Tamal* Tying Tool:

The tool is designed of a base of wood that is 4.5" long, 3.5" wide, and 0.75" thick. The upright wood ends are 3.25" tall, 3.5" wide, and 0.25" thick. The ends are nailed onto the base with small brads. As shown in the photo, cut a 'V' shape in each end piece, and add notches to the outer sides of the uprights. The "tails" of the *tamal* fit through the "V" in the uprights, allowing the *tamal* to be held in position for tying the tails. The notches give a bit of leverage when locking the string in place to wrap around the tails, keeping them tightly together while tying a narrow strip of husk around the tails, after which the string is removed, resulting in a nicely tied *tamal*!

The tool is very easy to make and the *tamal* fits perfectly between the upright ends of the tool. This helps keep the tamales a uniform size.

This tool was created by my Nana's godson, Arturo Owen Borboa, affectionately called Tootie. While at his home in Firebaugh one day, Tootie was showing me how to tie the tamales and he brought out this tool. I traced it on a page of yellow note paper—no phones for photos in those days! I took it home and my son made the wooden tool. My husband made it better for himself, for the actual tying of the tamales, by adding the notches on the four edges. The notches allow the string to be tightened before adding the cornhusk ties. Thanks to Tootie, it takes only one person to tie the tamales!!

Let's Start Cooking!

Step-by-step instructions with pictures to making a delicious batch of authentic *Californio* tamales

CHAPTER 5

Chile Pepper Purée

Make this first—the purée is used in all parts of the making of our *Californio*-style tamales!

Servings:
1 batch, about 1 quart (enough for 24 tamales, and "gravy" or sauce)

Ingredients:
- 10 California chile peppers, dried
- 6 Pasilla chile peppers, dried
- 1 garlic clove, chopped

Equipment:
- food-grade gloves
- 2 to 3 quart saucepan, with a lid
- blender (we use our Vita-Mix for a very smooth purée)
- 1 quart storage container, with a lid
- measuring cups (8 cup and ¼ cup sizes)

For this process <u>you should always wear gloves</u>. My brother didn't wear gloves once when he was helping me. Later in the day he changed his contact lens—and had several painful hours afterwards!

Steps:

1) Carefully remove the stems, seeds, and veins from the peppers and discard. Rinse the peppers well with cold water to remove the dust, dirt, and moldy spots. The seeds and veins produce the heat of the pepper. We remove almost all of them to keep our purée mild enough for most folks, but with a hint of heat for those who want it!

 Do not put the seeds, veins, and stems into a garbage disposer—they will jam it! Trust me, experience is talking here!

 While washing the broken-up peppers, they release oils carried into the air with the mist from the running water. Breathing this mist can be harmful to your lungs and eyes.

2) Break apart the peppers so they soften easily.

3) Place the broken pieces into the saucepan with enough water to just cover the peppers. Bring to a boil, then turn the heat down and simmer for 15 minutes. Let stand, covered, for at least an hour to soften the peppers.

4) Scoop a cup or so of the rehydrated peppers, along with about ¼ cup of the liquid and a few pieces of the chopped garlic clove, and put into a blender. Blend to a smooth purée and pour into a 1 quart measuring container.

5) Continue blending the remaining chiles with about ¼ cup of the pepper liquid for each batch along with pieces of the garlic until all have been puréed.
6) If this doesn't equal a full quart, just add a bit of the liquid from the peppers to make a full quart of the thick purée. For 24 tamales, you will need every drop of this purée!
7) Transfer to a quart-size storage container with a lid. If you're not using it now, the purée can be stored in the refrigerator for several weeks, or in the freezer for up to 6 months.

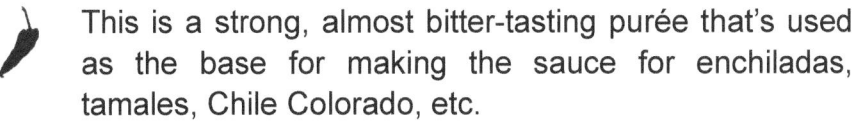 This is a strong, almost bitter-tasting purée that's used as the base for making the sauce for enchiladas, tamales, Chile Colorado, etc.

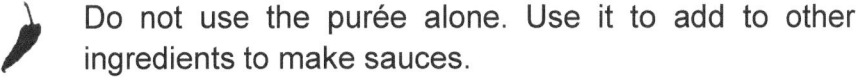 Do not use the purée alone. Use it to add to other ingredients to make sauces.

CHAPTER 6

Creating the BEST Sauce

This delicious sauce, a.k.a. tamale gravy, is so good on enchiladas, fajitas, beans, scrambled eggs, you name it! If you like the Mexican flavoring, you're gonna LOVE this sauce!

Servings:
about 2 quarts

Ingredients:
- 7 cups chicken broth, divided—reserve about a cup for the cornstarch slurry
- 1½ Tbsp. apple cider vinegar
- 1½ Tbsp. ground oregano
- 1½ Tbsp. ground cumin
- 1½ Tbsp. powdered Ancho chile
- 1 tsp. garlic powder
- 2 tsp. McCormick brand Montreal Steak Seasoning (or substitute with 2 tsp. salt and 1 tsp. pepper)
- 3 Tbsp. cornstarch

- 2 cups chile pepper purée

Equipment:
- 3 quart saucepan, with a lid
- 2 quart measuring container
- measuring cups (1 cup and 2 cup size)
- measuring spoons
- stirring spoon
- whisk

Steps:
1) Combine the chicken broth, vinegar, and spices in the saucepan, whisking well to blend.
2) Add cornstarch to the reserved chicken broth in a 2 cup measuring cup and whisk until it is a well-blended slurry. Add the slurry to the saucepan, whisking as it's being added so it stays smooth.
3) Stir in the purée and mix well.
4) Simmer for 20-30 minutes, stirring occasionally.
5) Strain to remove any particles of chile purée. Discard any solids.

 We put a few drops of the sauce into a glass of water to check for particles and often strain again so the final sauce is very clear. This step is important for a clear sauce so please take time to do it.

The sauce keeps well in the refrigerator for several weeks, tightly covered. Reheat on low for a few minutes, whisking to blend.

Serve over tamales, enchiladas, fajitas, or even scrambled eggs!

CHAPTER 7

Preparing the Meat Mixture

We use a combination of pork and beef for our regular tamales, or all beef for those who don't eat pork.

If you plan to make all beef tamales or all pork tamales, make sure the amount of meat totals 3.0 to 4.0 lbs. The rest of the ingredients and directions in this chapter are the same.

For one of our family tamale dinners, we had pork/beef tamales on one tray, all beef on another tray, just pork on a third tray, and our vegan tamales (see Chapter 13) on another tray! A lot of work but every family member at our table was able to share in our tamale dinner!

Servings:
about 24 tamales

Ingredients:
- 2.0 to 2.5 lbs pork—we use boneless Boston Butt roasts
- 1.0 to 1.5 lbs beef—we use boneless Chuck roasts
- Crisco shortening, about 2 Tbsp. per batch, or as needed

- 12 oz chicken broth—we use Swanson's brand low sodium
- 1 Tbsp. ground oregano
- 1 Tbsp. ground cumin
- 1 Tbsp. McCormick brand Montreal Steak seasoning (this is our go-to seasoning, a good blend of salt, pepper, etc.)
- 1½ tsp. garlic powder
- 1½ tsp. ground Ancho pepper
- 1¼ tsp. apple cider vinegar
- 2 cups chile pepper purée
- 3 Tbsp. cornstarch

Equipment:
- large pot—soup pot, stew pot, kettle, or something similar
- tongs
- large frying pan or sauté pan

Steps:
1) Cut the meat into stew-meat size cubes, trimming most of the fat and any muscle or gristle.
2) Working in batches, sear (brown) the cubes in hot oil until you get a good sear.
3) Place the seared meat into a large pot of water. Bring to a boil and then simmer for at least an hour.
4) Test a piece for doneness and when done, remove the meat from the water to cool.

5) When cool enough to work with, shred the meat either with your hands or two forks. Remove any remaining fat, muscle, and gristle in the meat. Set aside the shredded meat while you make the seasoning for it.

6) Whisk all the dry ingredients into the broth and vinegar, then add the cornstarch, stirring constantly. Continue to stir until all ingredients are well-blended.

7) Stir, don't whisk, in the chile pepper purée and mix well.

8) Pour over the shredded meat in a large pan, stir well, and heat on low for about 20 minutes.

9) Taste and add Montreal Steak seasoning or salt/pepper if needed.

CHAPTER 8

Corn Husks—or *Hojas de Maiz*

Corn husks are readily available in most grocery stores with ethnic aisles, or they can also be purchased on Amazon.

Servings:
about 24 tamales

Ingredients:
- 1 package (1 lb) corn husks

Equipment:
- Large container or bucket to soak corn husks
- Lid, smaller than the container or bucket, and something to weigh down the lid over the husks

Steps:
1) Remove and separate the tightly-packed husks.
2) Rinse the husks to remove dust and corn husk "strings" or dried silk strands.

3) Place the loose husks in a large container or bucket with enough hot water to cover them. Put a lid smaller than your container on the husks and keep the lid in place with some sort of weight on it to keep them under water. Let them soak while you make the masa.

4) When you're ready to begin making your tamales, separate the various sizes of husks, sorting them in stacks of the wide, large husks to smaller ones to dry on kitchen towels, not paper towels.

5) Using several of the very skinny husks, tear lengthwise strips, about ¼" to ½" wide, to be used for tying the ends of the tamales. Keep these strips damp until used.

CHAPTER 9

Mixing the Masa—the Fluffy, Blushing Tamale Dough

The delectable aroma experienced at the end of our tamale-making process is due almost entirely to the masa. The soft, fluffy, blush-colored tamale dough smeared on the husks, twice per *tamal*, is the best of the *tamal*! Chile purée added to the masa gives it such a nice color, and a subtle yet spicy flavor.

Servings:
about 24 tamales

Ingredients:

- 4 cups dry corn masa mix—we use Maseca brand Instant Corn Masa Mix for Tamales

 Be sure to use the Instant Corn Masa Mix for Tamales. Do not use Instant Corn Masa Flour for Tortillas!

- 2 tsp. baking powder
- 2 tsp. salt

- ½ cup chile pepper purée
- 4 cups chicken broth
- 9.2 oz Crisco shortening (weigh it!!)

Equipment:
- electric mixer—a hand-mixer works best
- a very large bowl, bigger than the bowl on a stand mixer
- measuring cups (¼, 2, 4, and 8 cup sizes)
- measuring spoons
- mixing spoons
- spatulas

Steps:
1) Begin by whipping the shortening in a bowl with an electric mixer <u>for a full 5 minutes</u>, until it's light, fluffy, and glossy.

2) Combine the dry masa and baking powder together in a large bowl and stir to mix well.

3) Put the broth, purée, and salt in a microwave-safe container and heat for 2-3 minutes until hot. Pour this hot liquid purée over the dry masa baking powder mix.

4) Using the electric mixer, combine the dry ingredients with the liquid until it is the consistency of smooth peanut butter. The purée gives the masa a nice reddish color and good flavor. If the masa is too thin, add a bit more dry masa. If the mixture is too thick, add a bit more broth until it looks and feels like smooth peanut butter.

5) Test your masa by putting a small teaspoon of the masa into a glass of room temperature water. If the masa floats then it's ready. If it sinks, it needs more shortening added and beating with the electric mixer for a few more minutes. Test again. The end result of fluffy cooked masa is well worth the time of testing.

 We smooth the top of the prepared masa in the bowl and draw lines with our masa spreader on the top of the masa, dividing the masa into sections, much like cutting a pie into equal pieces. This way we know we're putting the same amount of masa on each husk. We found this was helpful when we were talking too much and not paying close attention to what we were doing! If you're making 2 dozen tamales, make sure you have 24 wedges marked.

CHAPTER 10

Pennies in the Pot? Dancing Pennies?

The pennies in the pot let us know when the water level is low, and when we need to replenish it to prevent scorching our steamer.

Servings:
about 24 tamales

Ingredients:
- A few penny coins (we're serious!!)

Equipment:
- A deep pot will work, or if you have a tamale steamer, all the better!
- You will need some type of rack at the bottom of the pot to keep the tamales out of the water

Steps:
1) Fill the steamer with water to just below the rack, placing a couple of pennies on the bottom so you can hear them

"dancing" when the water is boiling. You don't want to run out of water in the pot!

2) We set up the pot before we begin to assemble the tamales and have the heat on low until we're almost ready to put the tamales into the pot.

CHAPTER 11

Tamalada—Tamales-Building Time!

We put three raisins and one pitted black olive in each of our *Californio* tamales. Why? It's tradition!

Servings:
about 24 tamales

Ingredients:

- 1 box or bag of raisins (at least 72 raisins)
- 1 can of pitted black olives (at least 24 olives)

Equipment:

- 1 *Tamal* Tying Tool
- food-grade cotton kitchen string—most grocery stores carry a version of the string, or you can find it on Amazon for less than $5
- baking sheet lined with paper towels for holding completed tamales, before placing them in a tamale pot

Steps:
Be sure to wear an apron and have plenty of towels available to wipe your hands and your work area. It's gonna get a bit messy! Watch out for small clumps of masa that have fallen on the floor!

Gather the utensils you'll be needing to spread the masa. We've found that a short, wide utensil once used in a wok works the best for us. Anything about 3" wide will work well, or even the back of a serving spoon!

Just before you begin, turn on the stove to low heat under the tamale pot. The water will be heating as you're making the tamales.

1) Put drained olives in a small container and a handful of raisins in another container near the person wrapping and tying the ends of the tamales so they can be added before the final wrapping. We always forget to add these to at least one, and it's fun to see who gets 'that' *tamal* at dinner!

2) If available, have your "*Tamal* Tying Tool" ready, along with a piece of food-grade kitchen string.

3) Place the seasoned meat mix in a bowl within reach of the person seated who will be adding the meat to the masa covered corn husks. You don't want to have to reach very far! We use a food scale, weighing each masa-covered husk as we add the meat, making certain we have a full 2 oz of meat in each *tamal*.

4) Count out 12 damp wider corn husks and 12 that are a bit narrower. Put these into two stacks on kitchen towels near the bowl of prepared masa.

For the next 2 steps, you need to find the <u>smooth</u> side of the damp husk. Yes, there is a smooth side and a rough side to the husk. Rub the husk on one of the nearby kitchen towels and you'll know which side is smooth and which side catches on the towel like "velcro." The smooth side allows the cooked masa to just slide off onto your plate!

5) Let's do it! With your spreader, spread masa, about 1/4" thick, down the middle of a wide husk, top to bottom, leaving about a 2" margin at the top and at the bottom without masa, and about an inch margin down the sides (lengthwise) of the husk so the masa doesn't squish out around the meat. This makes for a tidy bundle so the person doing the tying has room for the tie. And then they don't yell at you for making their job harder! And messy!

6) Scoop an ice-cream scooper full of meat and put it in the middle of the wider masa-smeared husk. We always add 2.0 ounces of meat mixture to a husk for each *tamal*, using a scale to check.

   Since the weight of just the masa and a husk (before adding the meat) varies depending on the size of the husk, first weigh the husk with its masa (perhaps it reads 1.8 ounces). After you add the meat mixture, the weight should be 2.0 ounces more (in our example shown in the next picture, the scale now reads 3.8 ounces).

   Once you have the desired amount of meat mixture added, pass the husk over to the person doing the wrapping and tying.

7) Smear another but narrower husk with masa and pass that one along too, but don't add meat to it. This husk is the outside "wrapper" that makes these tamales so delicious! Two layers of masa around the inner meat, raisins, and olive filling. Sometimes the "wrapper husk" tears, splits, or just doesn't do the job properly. No problem, just add another small masa-smeared husk over the split and ta-da! Split is fixed!

Remember, the person smearing masa and adding meat will need to smear one wide husk, add the 2 ounces of meat, then smear a narrower husk, not adding meat to this narrower husk, and then pass them on to the person doing the finish work.

8) The finish work is adding the olive and the three raisins on top of the meat mixture, folding the edges together, then laying the narrower husk, masa-smeared side down, over the seam of the folded edge of the meat-filled husk.

9) The *tamal*, with two layers of masa-smeared husks all wrapped together, is then placed in the "*Tamal* Tying Tool" with the tails of the *tamal* sticking out through the "V" in the uprights of the tool. This allows the tying of a narrow strip of husk around the tails. Please refer to the instructions at the end of Chapter 4.

10) As each tamal is tied, and thus completed, it is placed on a paper towel lined baking sheet. We put them in rows to count as the tamales are being readied for the tamale pot. Much easier to count at this stage than when trying to put down into the tamale pot!

11) We place the tamales around the outside edge of the tray in the bottom of the tamale pot, tail ends touching. Fill in the center with tamales touching tails. The next row up should be placed with the thicker part of the tamales over the tail ends, like stacking logs. Continue stacking the tamales in this same manner until all of your tamales are in the pot.

12) Place the lid on the tamale pot, turn the heat up to high, and listen for the pennies to dance! When the pennies begin to dance, turn the heat down to medium and continue to listen to the dancing pennies. This way you know there's still water in the pot steaming your tamales. If you no longer hear the pennies, add about 4 cups of hot water, pouring it down the inside walls of the tamale pot. The tamales should steam for about 2 hours. During the last 30 minutes or so you'll smell the delicious masa fragrance. They're almost ready!

13) When you think the tamales are ready, take one out and carefully unwrap it on a plate. The masa should look cooked, not gummy. If still a bit gummy, rewrap and place it back in the tamale pot and continue cooking for another 20–30 minutes.

14) Once the tamales are cooked, remove the lid—be careful, this steam is HOT and can cause serious burns!—and let the steam out of the pot. Using tongs, pick up each *tamal* by its tails and place on a tray to serve.

CHAPTER 12

Serving and Eating *Californio* Tamales

Corn husks, like the paper cups on the outside of cupcakes, are not to be eaten. They are the vessel in which the tamales are cooked. Please don't try to eat the husks!

1) Be sure to have heated sauce (tamale gravy) in containers, each on a saucer to prevent drips, on the table for your guests, you know, like your grandmother's gravy boat with a small ladle to serve the exact amount necessary on each hot tamale! If you're serving vegan tamales, be sure to clearly identify the container of vegan sauce for your guests.

2) We always let our guests snip, or slide, the ties off the ends of the tamales on their plate.

3) Carefully unwrap the individual tamales, taking in all of the deliciousness of what is in front of you!

4) Place the used corn husks and the ties in the container provided by your gracious host, such as a basket or bag. No one likes a pile of used husks sitting on the table in front of them, ick! Not to mention it dirties the tablecloth.

5) Enjoy, and bask in the raves from your guests! You deserve these compliments after all the work you've done during the past few days. Job well done!!

CHAPTER 13

Bonus Recipe: Vegan Tamales and Their Own Sauce

The ingredients we use for our vegan tamales will result in completely vegan food.

The differences in ingredients are noted throughout this recipe, such as replacing the chicken broth with vegetable broth. There are references back to previous chapters for instructions on how to complete the various steps.

Servings:
about 24 tamales

Chile pepper purée

Refer to Chapter 5! It's all the same for both regular and vegan tamales. If you want, you can start making your chile pepper purée and finish it while you are preparing the vegan black beans mixture.

Creating the vegan tamale sauce

Refer to Chapter 6, with a twist!

Replace the 7 cups of chicken broth with vegetable broth. All the other ingredients are the same.

The procedure is exactly the same, other than when the recipe and/or directions say, "chicken broth" you just think (and use) vegetable broth!!

This sauce keeps well in the refrigerator for several weeks, tightly covered. Reheat on low for a few minutes, whisking to blend.

If you freeze 2-cup quantities of the chile pepper purée in freezer bags, you'll be able to whip up a yummy sauce to serve over your favorite rice, beans, or any dish where you want a deep, delicious flavor!

Preparing the vegan black beans mixture

This section replaces Chapter 7 (which covered preparing the meat mixture for regular tamales).

Ingredients:
- 1 lb dried black beans sorted, rinsed and soaked overnight before cooking
- 4 bay leaves
- olive or avocado oil
- 6 large carrots, diced
- 1 large onion, chopped

- 5–6 large cloves garlic, chopped
- 1 can yellow or white hominy, drained, rinsed and soaked for 30 minutes in fresh water to remove more salt. Drain hominy again before using.

Spice mix:
- 4 Tbsp. ground cumin
- 1 Tbsp. powdered cocoa
- 4 Tbsp. mild chili powder (use what you like—ancho, etc.)
- 2 tsp. epazote
- 1 tsp. dried ground coriander
- 1 tsp. dried red pepper flakes

Equipment:
- No differences

Steps:
1) In a large pot, cover the beans with water, add bay leaves and bring to a boil. Reduce heat to a simmer and cover about halfway. Cook several hours until very tender. Drain but reserve the bean liquid, adding water to this liquid to total about a quart. Set aside the cooked beans.
2) In the large pot used to cook the beans, cook the onions, carrots, and garlic in 2-3 Tbsp. of olive or avocado oil. Cook until the carrots are softening, but not soft. Stir in the spice mix and coat the vegetables well. Cook for a few more minutes to let them absorb the spices.

3) Add the beans, hominy, and about 2½ cups of the reserved liquid. Cook on medium-high to reduce the liquid but carefully watch the mixture—it can stick to the bottom of the pan as it cooks down. As it does cook down, add more water/bean liquid and reduce again. You'll probably do this about three times, but you be the judge. Taste from time to time and add spices as needed but adjust the salt at the end after the mixture has reduced. The mixture should be thick, not soupy.

Corn husks—or *hojas de maiz*

Refer to Chapter 8 for preparing your corn husks.

Mixing the masa—the fluffy, blushing tamale dough

Refer to Chapter 9 for preparing the masa for your tamales!

We use Crisco shortening instead of lard in all of our *Californio* tamales recipes.

Replace the 4 cups of chicken broth with vegetable broth as you did when making the vegan tamale sauce.

All the other ingredients are the same.

Pennies in the pot? Dancing pennies?

Refer to Chapter 10, making certain your tamale steamer pot is set up with enough water!

Tamalada—tamales-building time!

And now the fun begins!! Refer to Chapter 11, except you will use the vegan black beans mixture instead of the meat mixture.

We probably sound a bit bossy in the chapter, but we want you to have the best time and enjoy the art of making the *Californio* tamales, even though here you are making vegan tamales!

If you didn't make, or have a handy friend make for you, our Handy-Dandy *Tamal* Tying Tool, go back to Chapter 4 and see the directions for making it! You'll be glad later that you have it to tie your tamales!

After all your hard work, and waiting about 2 hours for your tamales to steam, and smelling that *delicioso* aroma in your house during the last 30 minutes or so, it's time to eat your tamales! But how??

Well, first you carefully put the tamales on your plate from the steamer—use long tongs! **They're HOT**! Now either slide the ties from the ends or use a knife or scissors to clip the ties and remove them. Discard the ties.

Next, unwrap the very hot husk, slide the masa onto your plate, then unroll the inner husks and slide the very yummy filling and masa onto the masa already on your plate. Discard the used husks—they've done their duty.

Now the fun part—drizzle the sauce (a.k.a. "tamale gravy") over the top of your unwrapped tamale mixture and take a bite, savoring every flavor as your taste buds have a party in your mouth!!

CALIFORNIO TAMALES! AND SARSA!

The time, the effort, and maybe a frustration or two when tying the ends, was soooo worth that bite!

Enjoy!

CHAPTER 14
Californio Sarsa

Please read about our *Californio sarsa* at californioancestry.com/traditions-sarsa/.

Servings:
1 batch, about a quart, enough for great chip-dipping or for a sauce on just about everything!

Ingredients:

- 4 Anaheim chiles
- 2 jalapeno chiles, seeded!—some seeds are okay, too many, too hot!
- 5 or 6 firm tomatoes, Romas are my choice, but just about any home-grown tomato will do!
- 3–4 garlic cloves, smashed and minced
- 1 yellow onion, small, diced
- 2 Tbsp. olive oil
- 1–2 Tbsp. wine vinegar
- 1 tsp. fresh oregano or ½ tsp. dried oregano
- Salt to taste

- 2–3 Tbsp. snipped cilantro, optional—some folks just don't like cilantro!

Equipment:
- food-grade gloves
- long handle tongs
- 2-to-3-quart saucepan
- 1 quart storage container, with a lid

Steps:

 You should always wear gloves when doing steps 1 and 2.

 Do not put the seeds, veins, and stems into a garbage disposer—they will jam it! Trust me, experience is talking here!

1) Char the chiles over a gas flame or under a broiler until blackened. You might want to do this step outside on a BBQ grill. We set off our smoke alarm every time we do this in the kitchen!

2) After charring, steam the chiles for a few minutes in a paper bag (Nana wrapped them in a damp kitchen towel) or a plastic bag. With your gloved hands, rub the skin off under cold water but try not to breathe the mist—not healthy for your lungs! Cut off the tops from the chiles and remove veins and seeds. Chop into bite-size pieces.

3) Place whole tomatoes into rapidly boiling water for 30–45 seconds, then immediately into ice water. With a little help the skin will slip right off! Chop into bite-size pieces.

4) Combine all the ingredients in a saucepan. On medium heat, allow the *sarsa* mixture to simmer for about 20–30 minutes. Cool and store in the refrigerator.

We keep ours in a small container with a tight lid, like a jelly jar. Keeps refrigerated for about a week, but ours never lasts that long because we eat it! Serve with chips, over eggs, with anything!

A story, according to Mom and Dad, was that Dad used to drive Nana into town to get her peppers from a particular vendor. As the story goes, one time, again according to Mom and Dad, when Nana got her peppers home and began to sort them for use, she found a lot of mold, mildew, and dirt on them and she sorta flipped out. Dad had to drive her back into town or wherever the vendor was and Nana really let loose on the guy. Dad used to laugh when he told this story and said the poor guy just stood there with this tiny 4' 8" wild woman yelling at him in front of customers. Dad said Nana not only got her money back, but she also got additional peppers, for free!

About the Author

Sheila Ruiz Harrell, born in Madera, California, was raised in Modesto and has been interested in her ancestors, family, and the foods of her ancestors since she was a child—especially the food of her mother's side of the family—the *Californio* food!

Sheila is married with two adult children and three adult grandchildren who all share her love for the *Californio* tamales, and *sarsa* too!

California poppy on Highway 1. Photo courtesy of David Eppstein.

Sheila's reason for using images of the poppy, especially this one taken on Highway 1, is because it reminds her of how resilient and strong her ancestors were, both surviving and thriving in the harsh conditions of the new frontier of what would eventually become the State of California. This picture of the poppy made Sheila know that her ancestors were strong enough to thrive anywhere.

They did, and because of them, we are.

www.ingramcontent.com/pod-product-compliance
Lightning Source LLC
Chambersburg PA
CBHW042314150426
43200CB00001B/14